New Action Sports

Learning

Martial Arts

by Steve Potts

C A P S T O N E   P R E S S

M A N K A T O

C A P S T O N E   P R E S S
818 North Willow Street • Mankato, MN 56001

Printed in the United States of America.

Library of Congress Cataloging-in-Publication Data
Potts, Steve, 1956-
    Learning martial arts/Steve Potts
      p. cm.
    Includes bibliographical references (p. 46) and index.
    Summary: Gives a basic introduction to karate, judo, and ninjitsu.
    ISBN 1-56065-403-1
    1. Martial arts--Training--Juvenile literature. [1. Martial arts.] I. Title
GV1102.7 T7P68 1996
796.9--dc20   95-47163
                                                          CIP
                                                          AC

Photo credits
Peter Ford: cover, 4, 22, 32, 34
Unicorn Stock Photos/Dick Young: 6, 8, 12, 16, 26, 28, 42
Unicorn Stock Photos/Alon Reininger: 11
Unicorn Stock Photos/Chris Boylan: 14, 30
Unicorn Stock Photos/Paul Murphy: 19, 20, 24,
Archive Photos/John Bramley: 36
Unicorn Stock Photos/Ed Harp: 38
Unicorn Stock Photos/Sue Vanderbilt: 44

Table of Contents

Words in **boldface** type in the text are defined
in the Glossary in the back of this book.

Chapter 1
The Martial Arts

The martial arts are methods of self-defense. They blend both physical and mental conditioning. They began hundreds of years ago in China, Japan, Tibet, and India. Three of these arts are karate, judo, and ninjitsu.

Karate is currently the most popular martial art. Many communities offer karate classes.

Judo is popular with people of all ages, too. Judo emphasizes both conditioning and strength.

Ninjitsu is practiced by people called ninja. Because of their ability to hide themselves, ancient ninja seemed magical. Their skills made them the world's greatest secret agents. Television and movies have made them famous today.

Many communities offer classes in the martial arts.

Chapter 2

Karate

There are no weapons in karate. People use their bodies to perform kicks, blocks, and punches. There are two stories about the beginnings of karate.

Okinawa Beginning

One story says that karate started in Okinawa. This is an island southwest of Japan. Okinawa was settled more than 1,000 years ago by people from China.

Many of Okinawa's people, though, fought with the Chinese. In 1429, Okinawa's ruler told his soldiers to take away the people's weapons. All the swords, knives, and shields were

A good karate student controls both mind and body.

collected. They were stored in the ruler's castle.

In 1609, the Japanese came to Okinawa. They also banned all weapons. They said no one could fight against them.

Pirates and robbers often attacked the island people. But they had no way to defend themselves. They had no swords or knives. So they used their hands, feet, and heads.

They learned new ways to defend themselves. The skills they learned were called Okinawa-te. That means Okinawa-hands. Sometimes these skills were called kara-te, which means Chinese-hands.

India and China Beginning

The second story says that karate came from India and China. It says that a **Buddhist** monk from India brought karate to China in the year 520. He taught the Chinese monks exercises to

People can learn karate at any age. Many children participate in the martial arts.

control their breathing. He taught them ways to control their minds and bodies.

The monks learned from him. They taught karate as a mix of spirituality and self-defense.

Karate is still taught as a combination of these two ideas. A good karate student can control both mind and body.

Karate Training

A karate student is called a karateka. People can learn karate at any age. Many younger students compete in contests. These are held in many countries. Some older students learn karate to defend themselves. Others do it for the exercise.

Karate students practice in a dojo. This is a room with mats to practice on. Dojos have mirrors on the wall so students can watch themselves. This helps them learn kicks, **postures,** and movements.

Karate Belts

Karate students wear special clothes. Most karate outfits have loose-fitting pants and a

Karate techniques can be practiced in a wheelchair.

jacket. They are often white, but they may be
bright colors. A colored belt keeps the jacket
closed at the waist.

The belt's color tells what level a karateka is
at. Beginners wear a white belt. As students
master karate they can earn a yellow, orange,
green, purple, brown, or black belt.

A black belt is the highest rank in karate. A student must pass at least 10 tests to earn a black belt. Students who continue their training can earn up to 10 **degrees** within the black belt.

Karate Classes

The best way to learn karate is to take a class. Karate teachers must have at least a first-degree black belt. The best teachers are willing to work hard with their students. Learning karate is not easy. A good teacher helps students master the sport.

Karate classes usually have between five and 20 students. Most beginning classes are made up of students who are about the same age. Classes with both adults and younger people are popular at advanced levels.

Classes usually begin and end with stretching exercises. These exercises prepare students for a lesson. Stretching helps make sure the students do not pull or tear a muscle. At the end of the lesson, the exercises relax the muscles.

There are many belt levels in karate.

Chapter 3
Safe Techniques

Beginning karate students learn four basic **techniques.** They learn to punch, kick, strike, and block. Punching, kicking, and striking are offensive skills. Blocking is a defensive move.

Students do not actually hit or kick each other during class. They stop just before they make contact. A good kick or hit could cause an injury. Only in **full-contact competition** does a student make physical contact.

Stances, Punches, and Strikes

Each technique in karate uses a different stance. A stance is a special way to stand.

Students learn to switch between stances.

Students have to switch between stances. A stable stance is needed to do the rest of the moves.

Students throw punches with their arms and shoulders. They jerk their hips at the same time. This produces a forward thrust. Some of the first punches a student learns are straight, reverse, and lunge punches.

Students snap their elbows and forearms to strike. While striking, the elbow is relaxed and bent a little. The shoulder is also relaxed. Only the hand used to strike is kept firm.

Kicks and Blocks

Kicking is difficult to learn. It takes a lot of practice before the technique is mastered. Kicks have more power than punches or strikes with the hand.

To begin a kick, the foot is raised to the height of the opposite knee. The hands are raised to protect the face. The foot is snapped forward to complete the kick. It is then lowered

Kicks have more power than punches or strikes.

back to knee level. Successful kicks require a stable stance and good muscle control.

Blocking protects a student against punches, strikes, and kicks. In karate class you learn to use your body to block moves. You learn to put your body in a position after a block to deliver punches, strikes, and kicks.

Learning to Fall

It is important to learn how to fall correctly. This will protect you from injury. Students are taught to fall on the mat as hard as possible. The mat, not the body, absorbs the fall.

Students learn never to fall on their spine. They learn to tuck in their head. That way the most important parts of the body are not hurt.

Karate Matches

Advanced karate students often enter competitions. They choose between point fighting and full-contact karate.

Karate students of all ages participate in competitions.

In point fighting, no contact is made. Students wear protective gloves and shoes in case contact is accidentally made. A student scores points if a kick, punch, or strike reaches but does not touch a vital area.

In full-contact karate, students wear boxing gloves and special footwear. They kick and punch to score points. Opponents knock each other to the mat. Sometimes they even knock each other out.

Tournament divisions are based on students' level of skill. The divisions are beginner, intermediate, advanced, and expert. Three to five judges score the participants. The judges are black belt experts. Many tournaments offer individual, group, and team events.

Successful kicks require a stable stance and good muscle control.

Chapter 4

Judo

Judo originated in China and Japan. It was known as jujitsu. This means the gentle art. It was an early form of wrestling in China.

By the early 1600s, jujitsu was brought to Japan. It was adopted by the samurai. These warriors fought for Japanese warlords.

Samurai fought on horseback and on foot. They used swords, knives, and bows and arrows. Sometimes they lost their weapons or their horses were killed during a battle. When

The judoist on the right is preparing to drop her opponent.

that happened, they needed another way to fight. That way was jujitsu.

Modern Judo

In the 1880s, a young Japanese man turned the ancient art of jujitsu into modern judo. His name was Jigoro Kano.

Kano studied with one of the best teachers in Japan. Then he changed some of the old techniques. He added some karate techniques. Kano called his method judo.

Judo became very popular in Japan. Judo demonstrations were held in the United States and England.

Several famous people watched the exhibitions, including U.S. presidents Ulysses S. Grant and Theodore Roosevelt. Roosevelt even brought a judo teacher to the White House in Washington, D.C. The teacher gave lessons to Roosevelt and his son.

Karate and judo students practice in a dojo.

Fair Play

Kano emphasized the idea of fair play. He thought students should take care of each other. He thought it was a disgrace for someone with advanced skills to hurt someone who was a beginner. Kano wanted a martial art that could help people and improve society.

The Gi and Belts

Kano's students wore a white uniform called a gi. A gi has a thick, quilted jacket to absorb falls. It has loose pants that look like pajamas. The pants let students move freely.

The gi is made of heavy fabric. It can take many rough practices. The jacket closes with a belt. Just like in karate, the belts are different colors. Each color represents a rank or level of progress. Each of these ranks has levels. The black belt, for example, has 12 different levels.

In Japan, judo students can earn white, brown, and black belts. In North America and

Different colored belts represent levels of progress.

Europe, judo classes have added yellow, green, orange, and blue belts.

The Dojo

Kano wanted his students to learn how to fall without getting hurt. Like karate students, judo students practice in a dojo. The floors are covered with mats so students do not hurt themselves when they fall.

Dojo means place for learning the way. Most judo dojos have a picture of Kano hanging in the practice room. This reminds students of his dedication to the martial arts.

Tournament divisions are based on students' skill levels.

Chapter 5

Safe and Respectful

When students begin a judo class, everyone bows before walking onto the mat. Bows are a way of saying hello. They are also a sign of respect.

Students line up according to their rank. They kneel in front of their teacher. They bow to Kano's picture. Next, they bow to their teacher who is called a sensei. This means teacher in Japanese. Students also bow to each other before and after a session.

The martial arts blend physical and mental conditioning.

Judo students take time for warm-up exercises. Judo uses many muscles. Students must stretch and relax before practice so these muscles are not pulled or hurt.

Judo Techniques

Judo students are called judoka. The first thing they do is ukemi. Ukemi is falling practice. Students learn to fall forward, backward, and to the sides. These special ways to fall are called breakfalls. Students also practice rolling out of the falls.

Next students learn how to throw each other. The Japanese word for these throwing methods is nage-waza. The art of judo depends on making your opponents lose their balance.

Judo students push, pull, and twist their opponents to make them lose their balance. Then they throw them to the mat.

There are special ways to throw people in judo. There are many different kinds of throws. Which throw is used depends on the situation.

There are special ways to throw people in judo.

Control on the Mat

If a throw is successful, the opponent falls to the mat. Then the student holds, chokes, and locks the opponent to the mat. This kind of mat work is called katame-waza.

There are special rules for mat work. Poking eyes and biting are forbidden. Chokes are used carefully. If opponents cannot breathe, they tap their hands twice on the mat. This is called a tap out. It means they give up.

Chokes and locks can be dangerous. They are not used by beginning students.

Judo students push, pull, and twist their opponents to make them lose their balance.

Chapter 6
Ninjitsu

A famous Chinese general was **Sun-tze.** He wrote about ninja tactics almost 2,000 years ago. In the sixth century, the tactics were brought to Japan from China. Warriors who lived in Japan's mountains studied the ways of the ninja.

Ninja were the first secret agents. Japanese warlords hired the ninja to go into enemy camps. They spied and escaped with information. The weapons and secret tricks they used made the ninja famous.

The popular Teenage Mutant Ninja Turtles are based on the famous Japanese ninja.

Martial arts tournaments offer individual, group, and team events.

The ninja were very secretive. Most of what we know about them comes from legends. Sometimes it is hard to know what is true and what is false. The ancient ninja wanted it that way. They could do their jobs best when people knew nothing about them.

Ninja Training

Only a few families practiced ninjitsu. The secret techniques were passed down through the generations. The ninja families lived in the mountains. They kept their identity hidden.

Boys and girls began ninja training when they were five years old. They learned to swim, climb, jump, run, and ride horses. Some ninja could run for two or three days without resting.

Ninja learned to control their bodies. They learned to hold their breath for long periods. They had to remain hidden when they spied. They learned to stay still and not move, sometimes for a whole day. The last thing they learned was how to use weapons.

Secrecy and Magic

Few people knew who the ninja were. Ninja often changed their names and jobs to keep their secrets. One day, the ninja might be disguised as fishermen. The next day, the same ninja might dress up as dancers. They lived in houses with hidden rooms, underground hiding places, and secret doors.

Ninja used magic to frighten their enemies. Some people believed ninja could turn themselves into animals. Ninja learned magic to hide themselves. They hid underwater, breathing through a bamboo reed. Many people thought they were invisible.

The color of their clothes helped them stay hidden. They wore dark brown at night. During the winter they wore white or gray. Sometimes ninja hid under a cape on the ground. They also hid in trees, crawling close to the branches.

Ninja Techniques

Ninja knew many techniques to spy on their enemies. When they were children, ninja learned special ways to move the joints in their arms, legs, and hands. This helped them untie knots and escape when they were tied with ropes. They used small tools hidden in their clothes and hair to open locks.

Water did not scare the ninja. They used special boats to cross rivers. Life jackets and special shoes helped them float. Ninja seemed to use magic to cross over water, but it was just their training and special tools.

Ninja were famous for being able to climb anything. They used their hands and feet. They used ropes, ladders, metal hooks, and claws to creep up the sides of castles.

When ninja had to jump off high buildings, they used their capes or shirts as parachutes. They also flew on kites from the tops of buildings to the ground.

Ninja Weapons

Ninja learned martial arts and used many weapons. They were masters of a type of sword fighting called kenjutsu.

They learned how to use a bow and arrow and a long rod called a staff. Sometimes ninja hid a knife or chain in the staff to surprise their enemies.

When they attacked, ninjas rubbed arrow tips with oil and set them on fire. They shot the arrows into enemy towns, setting houses on fire.

Ninja threw a star-shaped weapon to the ground. The sharp points stuck in the enemy's feet to slow them down. Sometimes ninja threw the star directly at people.

Ninja also used chemicals. They put poison on darts and shot them through **blowguns.** They blew powder through tubes to blind the enemy.

Some chemicals were put into food. These could put people to sleep or kill them. Ninja also liked to make people laugh, cry, or itch with their powders.

Modern Ninja

Secrecy was important to the ancient ninja. But today anyone who wants to can learn ninjitsu. Modern ninja are not spies anymore.

Modern ninja learn in dojos, just like karate and judo students. Masaaki Hatsumi is the most famous modern ninja leader. His dojo is in Japan.

The modern ninja want to use their art to become better people. They want to use the ninja ways to help society. They are not much like the ancient ninja at all.

Kicking is hard to learn. It takes a lot of practice before the technique is mastered.

Glossary

blowguns—long, tubelike weapon through which darts are blown

Buddhist—a person who practices Buddhism, one of the most important religions and philosophies in China, Japan, Korea, and Southeast Asia

degrees—different ranks or positions within something

full-contact competition—karate match where competitors kick and hit

postures—the way a person stands

Sun-tze—Chinese general who wrote about ninja tactics and warfare almost 2,000 years ago in *The Art of War*

techniques—the way a person uses their skills to make something artistic or to make something happen

Parents and children can enjoy the martial arts.

To Learn More

Finn, Michael. *Martial Arts: A Complete Illustrated History.* Woodstock, N.Y.: The Overlook Press, 1988.

Gutman, Bill. *Judo.* Minneapolis: Capstone Press, 1995.

Gutman, Bill. *Karate.* Minneapolis: Capstone Press, 1995.

Metil, Luana, and Jace Townsend. *The Story of Karate: From Buddhism to Bruce Lee.* Minneapolis: Lerner Publications, 1995.

Neff, Fred. *Lessons From The Samurai: Ancient Self-Defense Strategies and Techniques.* Minneapolis: Lerner Publications, 1987.

Winderbaum, Larry. *The Martial Arts Encyclopedia.* Washington, D.C.: Inscape Corporation, 1977.

Useful Addresses

American Judo Association
P.O. Box 1568
Santa Barbara, CA 93102

Judo Canada
1600 James Naismith Drive
Ottawa, ON K1B 5N4
Canada

United States Judo Federation
21054 Sarah Hills Drive
Saratoga, CA 95070

U.S. Karate Federation
1300 Kenmore Road
Akron, OH 44314

You can read about martial arts in *Black Belt* magazine.

Index